Contents

Stalin

Sandra Woodcock

Published in association with The Basic Skills Agency

Hodder & Stoughton

A MEMBER OF THE HODDER HEADLINE GROUP

Acknowledgements

Photos: pp. 9, 15, 24 © Hulton Deutsch Collection,
        pp. 13, 26 © Hulton Getty Collection, p. 20 © Corbis.
Cover photo: © Popperfoto.
Artwork: pp. 2–3 © Lineart.

Orders: please contact Bookpoint Ltd, 39 Milton Park, Abingdon, Oxon OX14 4TD. Telephone: (44) 01235 400414, Fax: (44) 01235 400454. Lines are open from 9.00–6.00, Monday to Saturday, with a 24 hour message answering service. Email address: orders@bookpoint.co.uk

British Library Cataloguing in Publication Data
A catalogue record for this title is available from The British Library

ISBN 0 340 71161 2

First published 1998
Impression number 10 9 8 7 6 5 4 3 2 1
Year 200? 2002 2001 2000 1999 1998

Typeset by Fakenham Photosetting Ltd, Fakenham, Norfolk.
Printed in Great Britain for Hodder & Stoughton Educational, a division of Hodder Headline Plc, 338 Euston Road, London NW1 3BH by Page Bros Ltd, Norwich.

When Stalin was born,
Russia was an empire ruled by
one man – the Tsar.
The country was backward.
It was way behind Britain and Germany.
Most of the Russians were poor peasants.

Stalin began life as a peasant
and became ruler of Russia.
By the time he died,
Russia was a Superpower.
It had become a rival to the USA.

What part did Stalin play in all of this?

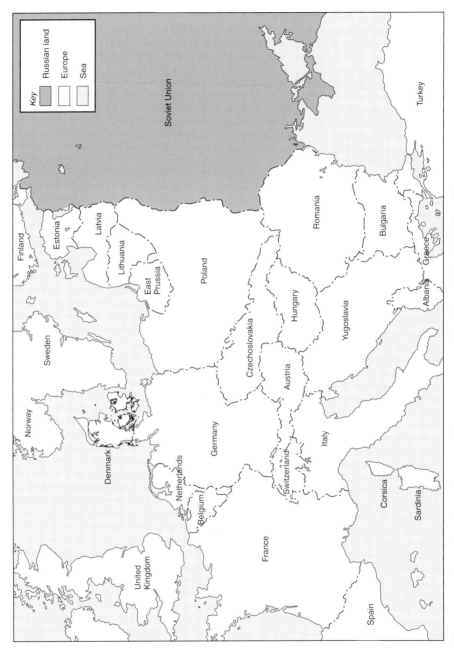

Europe, showing borders as they appeared before World War II.

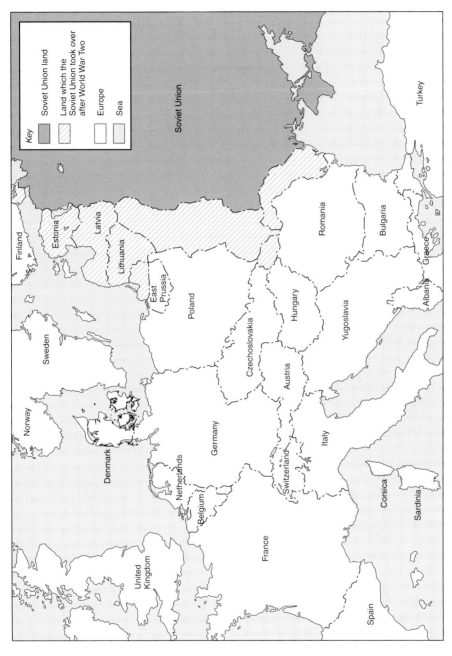

Europe, showing land which the Soviet Union took over after World War II.

1 The Son of a Peasant

Joseph was born into a poor family.
At first he was not called Stalin.
He took that name later.
His real name was
Iosif Vissarionovich Dzhugashvili.

His father was a shoe maker.
His mother had to work as a washer woman
so that they could live.

They were peasants.
The family home was a humble shack.
They had a kitchen and one other room.

Joseph's father was moody and cruel
to his wife and son.
He would often beat the boy.
When Joseph was 11, his father died.

Joseph's mother wanted him
to become a priest.
She sent him to a church school
and he did well there.

He was quick to learn.
Some of the other boys looked down on him
because he was so poor.

But Joseph could do better than them
at most things.
Soon he was bossing them all.

When he left school,
he went to a college.
He wanted to train as a priest.
His mother did not have to pay
because he was so clever.

Joseph and the other students
had to live like monks.
They had to stay in the college
all day and all night.
They could only read college books.
But they got hold of many books
from outside the college.

2 The Communist

Joseph was interested in politics.
He wanted Russia to change.
He wanted the poor to have a better deal.
He wanted the Tsar to give up his power.
He wanted the people to have more power.

Joseph read books by Karl Marx,
and he became a Communist.
The Communists wanted a
revolution in Russia.

Joseph was expelled from college
because he broke the rules.
He went out when he was told not to.
He read books which were banned.
He left the college
and gave up the plan to be a priest.

He met up with other Communists.
He met a man called Lenin.
Lenin was the leader of the Communists.

The Communists went to
the factory workers.
They told the workers that the
bosses were cheating them.
They said it was wrong that
workers had such low wages.
They said the workers should go on strike.

In Russia at that time,
people who tried to change things
were seen as dangerous.
The police were always on the look out
for Communists.

Many of them were arrested.
The Communists had to use code names,
because of the police.

The Communists gave Joseph
a code name – Stalin.
It means 'man of steel'.
For the rest of his life,
he was known as Joseph Stalin.

Stalin (left) with Lenin (right).

Stalin was arrested eight times.
He managed to escape six times.
Each time he escaped, he went back
to work for the Communists.

He planned a bank robbery
to get funds for them.

The Communists did not do well in Russia.
They were a tiny group
in a huge empire.
The people did not understand
their ideas.

Lenin, the leader of the Communists, said:
'There will not be a revolution
in our lifetime.'

But he was wrong.

3 Revolution

In 1914, Russia went to war.
The First World War was too much for Russia.
The Tsar and his government
could not cope.

People were short of food.
Soldiers were short of weapons.
Many did not even have boots to wear.

Workers went on strike.
The Tsar gave up.
He could not go on as leader of Russia.

A new government took over.
But Lenin and the Communists
were still not happy.
They wanted to be the leaders of Russia.

They waited for their chance.
The new government did not end the war.

One night, in October 1917,
a small group of Communists took over
all the main buildings in the capital city.
Stalin was not there.
He was in prison in Siberia.

The next morning,
Lenin told the people of Russia
that the Communists were their new leaders.
The Communists took Russia
out of World War 1.
Stalin left prison and joined Lenin.

Now that the Communists were in control,
things in Russia changed.
The rich people had to give up their land.
The Tsar and his family were killed.
New leaders were put in charge
all over Russia.

But life was still very hard for people.
The Communists were harsh and cruel
to people who did not agree with them.

Lenin looked for people he could
trust and depend on.
He gave power to these people.
He trusted Stalin and gave him a lot of power.

Revolution!

4 The Leader

Stalin was clever and cunning.
He kept in the background
but he controlled a lot of people.

When Lenin died in 1924,
Stalin wanted to be the new leader.

He plotted against his rivals.
The Communist Party was split.
Stalin would take first one side
and then the other.

His main rival was a man called
Leon Trotsky.
Stalin turned the rest of the Communists
against Trotsky.
They sent Trotsky out of Russia.

Leon Trotsky.

Trotsky had to hide from Stalin's men
for the rest of his life.
He lived in different countries.
He wrote books against Stalin.

Trotsky was a long way from Russia,
but Stalin was still afraid of him.
At last, in 1940,
one of Stalin's men found Trotsky in Mexico.
He killed him with an ice pick.

By 1929, Stalin was in control of Russia.
No-one except Trotsky had dared
to go against him.

Stalin said that Russia
was way behind other countries.
He wanted to bring Russia up to date.

He said there must be
more factories, more industry.
Stalin said the farmers must pay for this.
He said they must hand over
most of their corn and meat
to the government.

5 Fear and Terror

Stalin said farmers had to give up
their own farms.
They had to work for farms
run by the government.
Many farmers refused to do it.

But Stalin sent soldiers to the villages.
They had machine guns.
They were given orders to shoot farmers
who would not do as they were told.

Stalin sold most of Russia's corn
to other countries.
Russian people starved.
There was a famine.

People ate dogs and cats.
They even ate the bodies of dead people.
Seven million people died.

Stalin would not let the press
report the famine.
He was making money to use for industry.

He set targets for the people.
They had to make much more steel.
They had to dig more coal.
They had to build more railways
and power stations.
More of everything.

They had to catch up with the USA.
There were strict new rules.

A worker would lose his job
if he took one day off.
If a worker was twenty minutes late,
he had part of his wages taken away.
If a worker left his job,
he could be put in prison.
Workers could be put to death
for stealing property from the State.

The plans worked.
Stalin made Russia into a modern State.
But he had used force to do it.

Many people said he was
doing everything too fast.
The people were suffering
His own wife was upset by the famine.

She spoke out against him.
Then she killed herself.
Yet Stalin always kept cool.
His face never showed what he was thinking.
It was as if he wore a mask.

Stalin never felt safe.
He was always afraid
someone would try to kill him,
or take his place as the leader.

He spent all his time in the Kremlin.
He was not often seen in public.
But his picture hung in every work place.

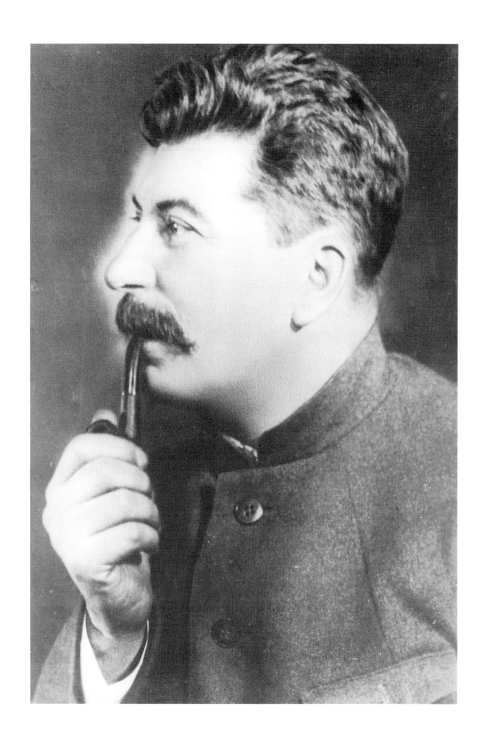

Stalin was afraid of people who might be
better than he was.
He would arrest them
and have them killed.

Millions died because of his fears.
They were called enemies of Russia.
They were sent to slave labour camps
and worked to death.

Stalin got rid of some of the
best men in Russia.

The people were ruled by fear.

Stalin was also afraid of other countries.
He was afraid of Germany,
and its leader, Adolf Hitler.
In 1939 he made a treaty with Hitler,
to avoid a war with Germany.

But in 1941, Hitler ordered
Germany to go to war with Russia anyway.
German armies invaded.

Now Stalin had to be a war leader.

6 War

In the war against Hitler,
Russia was very important.
The Russians kept the German armies
at bay for many years.

Stalin took charge of the war.
He said the Russians must fight
to the last man.
They must not give in to the Germans.

Stalin's own son was taken prisoner
by the Germans.
The Germans offered to hand his son back,
but Stalin refused.
He thought that his own son could
be a spy for the Germans.
Instead, Stalin had his son's wife
arrested and killed.
Stalin's son was killed by the Germans
two years later.

The Russians fought bravely
and won an important battle at Stalingrad.

Twenty million Russians
died in the Second World War.
That was far more than any other country.

Stalin was now a world leader.
He met other world leaders,
Winston Churchill from Britain,
and Franklin Roosevelt from America.
They all planned how to beat Hitler.

They also had to plan what to do in Europe
once the war was over.
Russian armies were in Germany.
They were in many other countries
in Eastern Europe.

Stalin did not trust Britain and America.
He said Russia must be safe
in years to come.
At the end of the Second World War,
Stalin would not agree to take
Russian armies out of Eastern Europe.

Stalin (left), Roosevelt (centre) and Churchill (right).

All the countries in Eastern Europe
became Communist.
Russia was cut off from
the rest of the world.

Still he did not feel safe.
He was always afraid.
He still talked about plots and traitors.
People still lived in fear of
'the man of steel'.

When Stalin died in 1953,
many people were glad.

But others said he had been
a great leader for Russia.
Stalin had made Russia into
a Superpower.
He did not care that millions
of people had died.
To him, it was a price that had to be paid.